Brian

Mulroney

Architect of

Transformation

Mathew Manuel

Comprehensive reads.

Brian Mulroney's Biography

A Captivating Biography of Canada's Influential Prime Minister

Table of Content

<u>Introduction</u>

Brian Mulroney stands as one of the most significant figures in Canadian political history, leaving an indelible mark on the nation's landscape. Born on March 20, 1939, in Baie-Comeau, Quebec, Mulroney's journey from a humble upbringing to the highest office in the land is a testament to his determination, charisma, and political acumen.

As the 18th Prime Minister of Canada, serving from September 17, 1984, to June 25, 1993, Mulroney's tenure was marked by bold initiatives, sweeping reforms, and transformative policies that reshaped the nation's trajectory. His leadership of the Progressive Conservative Party propelled him into office with one of the largest parliamentary majorities in Canadian history, a testament to his ability to resonate with the Canadian electorate.

The purpose of this biography is to provide a comprehensive and detailed exploration of Brian Mulroney's life, from his early years in Quebec to his rise to power and his enduring legacy. By delving into his personal background, political career, policy decisions, and lasting impact, we aim to offer readers a nuanced understanding of this enigmatic and influential leader.

Through meticulous research, firsthand accounts, and historical analysis, this biography seeks to uncover the man behind the politician, shedding light on both his triumphs and tribulations. From his landmark free trade agreement with the United States to his efforts to address pressing social issues, Mulroney's legacy reverberates through Canadian politics to this day.

As we embark on this journey through the life of Brian Mulroney, we invite readers to join us in exploring the complexities of his character, the challenges he faced, and the enduring imprint he left on the fabric of Canadian society.

Chapter 1: Early Life and Education

Family Background and Upbringing:

Brian Mulroney was born on March 20, 1939, in Baie-Comeau, Quebec, Canada, to an Irish Catholic family. His father, Benedict Mulroney, worked as an electrician, while his mother, Irene (née O'Shea), was a homemaker. Brian was the third of four children, growing up alongside his siblings, three brothers.

The Mulroney family lived modestly, and young Brian learned the values of hard work, determination, and perseverance from an early age. His parents instilled in him a strong sense of community and faith, which would shape his character and guide him throughout his life.

Despite facing financial challenges, the Mulroney household was filled with love, laughter, and a deep sense of camaraderie. Brian's parents emphasized the importance of education and encouraged their children to excel academically, setting the stage for Brian's future pursuits.

Education and Early Influences:

Brian Mulroney attended St. Thomas High School in Chatham, New Brunswick, where he distinguished himself as a diligent student and natural leader. He excelled academically and actively participated in extracurricular activities, including debate club and student government.

After graduating from high school, Mulroney pursued higher education at St. Francis Xavier University in Antigonish, Nova Scotia. There, he continued to excel both academically and socially, immersing himself in campus life and forging lifelong friendships.

It was during his time at St. Francis Xavier that Mulroney's interest in politics began to blossom. Inspired by the ideals of public service and civic engagement, he became involved in student politics and honed his oratory skills through debates and public speaking engagements.

Mulroney's time at university also exposed him to a diverse range of perspectives and ideologies, shaping his political worldview and laying the groundwork for his future career in public service.

As he embarked on his journey into adulthood, Brian Mulroney emerged from his formative years with a strong sense of purpose, armed with the values instilled by his family and the knowledge gained through his education. Little did he know that his experiences during these early years would pave the way for a remarkable journey in Canadian politics and leadership.

Chapter 2: Early Career and Entry into Politics:

Mulroney's Professional Career Before Entering Politics:

Before venturing into the realm of politics, Brian Mulroney pursued a successful career in law and business, laying the foundation for his eventual ascent to the highest office in Canada.

After completing his law degree at Laval University in Quebec City, Mulroney articled with a prominent law firm in Montreal, where he gained valuable experience in corporate law and litigation. His sharp intellect, strong work ethic, and natural charisma quickly set him apart, earning him recognition and respect within the legal community.

In 1965, Mulroney joined the prestigious law firm of Coudert Brothers in Montreal, where he specialized in labor law and quickly rose through the ranks to become a partner. During his time at Coudert Brothers, Mulroney handled high-profile cases and represented numerous corporate clients, further solidifying his reputation as a skilled and capable attorney.

In addition to his legal career, Mulroney also ventured into the business world, serving on the board of directors for several companies and leveraging his expertise to advise on matters of corporate governance and strategy.

Motivations for Entering Politics:

Despite his success in law and business, Brian Mulroney felt a calling to public service and sought to make a more significant impact on the world around him. Inspired by his upbringing, his education, and his deep-rooted sense of duty to his country, Mulroney made the decision to enter the arena of politics.

Mulroney was drawn to the Progressive Conservative Party of Canada, attracted by its principles of fiscal responsibility, social progress, and national unity. He saw politics as a means to effect positive change and address the pressing issues facing Canada, from economic stagnation to regional disparities.

Driven by a desire to serve his fellow Canadians and guided by his strong moral compass, Mulroney embarked on a new chapter in his life, leaving behind the comforts of his legal and business career to pursue a path of public service.

His decision to enter politics was not taken lightly, but Mulroney was undeterred by the challenges that lay ahead. With unwavering determination and a clear vision for the future, he set his sights on the highest office in the land, ready to lead Canada into a new era of prosperity and opportunity.

Little did Brian Mulroney know that his foray into politics would catapult him onto the national stage, where he would leave an indelible mark on Canadian history and shape the course of the nation for years to come.

Chapter 3: Leadership of the Progressive Conservative Party

Rise Within the Party Ranks:

Brian Mulroney's ascent within the Progressive Conservative Party (PC) of Canada was a testament to his political skill, strategic acumen, and ability to connect with voters across the country.

Mulroney's journey to the leadership of the PC Party began with his involvement in party politics at the grassroots level. He tirelessly campaigned for local candidates, built relationships with party members, and worked his way up through the ranks, earning the trust and respect of his colleagues along the way.

In 1976, Mulroney made his first bid for political office, seeking the PC nomination in the riding of Central Nova. Although unsuccessful in his initial attempt, he remained undeterred and continued to build support within the party.

In 1978, Mulroney's perseverance paid off when he was appointed as the President of the PC Party of Canada, a position that allowed him to expand his influence and shape the party's direction. His leadership skills and organizational prowess were on full display as he worked tirelessly to strengthen the party's infrastructure and mobilize support for future electoral campaigns.

Mulroney's star continued to rise within the party, and in 1983, he emerged as the frontrunner in the race for the PC leadership. With his dynamic personality, commanding presence, and compelling vision for the future, he captured the hearts and minds of party members across the country, securing a decisive victory in the leadership contest.

Campaigns and Strategies for Leadership:

Brian Mulroney's campaigns for the leadership of the PC Party were marked by innovation, strategic thinking, and a relentless focus on connecting with voters.

Recognizing the importance of grassroots support, Mulroney embarked on a cross-country tour, crisscrossing Canada to meet with party members, engage with local communities, and rally support for his candidacy. His energetic campaign style and ability to relate to Canadians from all walks of life resonated with voters, positioning him as a formidable contender for the party leadership.

In addition to his personal charisma, Mulroney employed a range of innovative campaign strategies to differentiate himself from his competitors and appeal to a broad spectrum of voters. From televised debates to targeted advertising campaigns, he leveraged every available platform to articulate his vision for the party and the country.

Central to Mulroney's campaign was his commitment to unity, prosperity, and national renewal. He spoke passionately about the need to revitalize Canada's economy, strengthen national unity, and restore confidence in government. His message struck a chord with Canadians weary of political discord and economic uncertainty, propelling him to victory in the leadership race.

With his election as leader of the Progressive Conservative Party, Brian Mulroney embarked on a new chapter in his political career, poised to lead the party to victory in the upcoming federal election and usher in a new era of conservative leadership in Canada.

Chapter 4: Prime Ministership (I)

Election to Prime Minister in 1984

Brian Mulroney's election as Prime Minister of Canada in 1984 marked the beginning of a transformative era in Canadian politics. His landslide victory over the incumbent Liberal government under Pierre Trudeau signaled a seismic shift in the country's political landscape and set the stage for ambitious reforms and initiatives.

The Campaign:

The 1984 federal election campaign was one of the most closely watched and hotly contested in Canadian history. Brian Mulroney, buoyed by his dynamic leadership and ambitious policy platform, led the Progressive Conservative Party into battle against the ruling Liberal Party, which had governed Canada for almost two decades.

Mulroney's campaign was marked by a sense of optimism and renewal, as he promised to revitalize Canada's economy, strengthen national unity, and restore trust in government. He crisscrossed the country, delivering impassioned speeches, shaking hands, and engaging directly with voters from coast to coast.

Key issues in the campaign included Mulroney's pledge to renegotiate the terms of the Canada-U.S. Free Trade Agreement, which he argued would stimulate economic growth and create jobs. He also emphasized the need for fiscal responsibility and accountability, promising to rein in government spending and tackle the country's mounting debt.

Despite facing fierce opposition from the Liberals and skepticism from some quarters, Mulroney's message resonated with Canadians weary of economic stagnation and political gridlock. His charismatic personality, combined with a meticulously planned campaign strategy, propelled him to victory on election day.

The Landslide Victory:

On September 4, 1984, Canadians headed to the polls to cast their ballots in what would prove to be a historic election. When the votes were tallied, Brian Mulroney and the Progressive Conservative Party emerged victorious in a landslide victory, capturing 211 of the 282 seats in the House of Commons.

The scale of Mulroney's triumph was unprecedented, with the PC Party winning the largest majority in Canadian parliamentary history. The Liberal Party, led by John Turner, was decimated, reduced to a mere 40 seats and relegated to opposition status.

Mulroney's victory was a watershed moment in Canadian politics, signaling a clear mandate for change and a rejection of the status quo. His landslide win reflected widespread dissatisfaction with the Liberal government's handling of the economy, as well as a desire for new leadership and fresh ideas.

The Mulroney Era Begins:

With his election as Prime Minister of Canada, Brian Mulroney embarked on a bold agenda to transform the country and tackle the pressing challenges facing Canadians. From economic reform to constitutional negotiations, his tenure in office would be defined by ambitious initiatives and hard-fought battles, shaping the course of Canadian history for years to come.

As the Mulroney era began, Canadians looked to their new leader with hope and optimism, eager to see how he would deliver on his promises and lead the country into a brighter future. Little did they know that the coming years would be filled with triumphs, controversies, and defining moments that would leave an indelible mark on the fabric of Canadian society.

Chapter 5: Prime Ministership (II)

Major Policies and Initiatives During His Tenure

Brian Mulroney's tenure as Prime Minister of Canada from 1984 to 1993 was characterized by a series of bold policies and initiatives aimed at revitalizing the economy, strengthening national unity, and positioning Canada as a global leader. Despite facing numerous challenges and controversies, Mulroney's government left an indelible mark on the country's political landscape.

1. Economic Reform:

Central to Mulroney's agenda was the pursuit of economic reform and modernization. His government implemented a series of bold policies aimed at stimulating growth, reducing deficits, and promoting free trade.

One of Mulroney's most significant achievements was the negotiation and implementation of the Canada-U.S. Free Trade Agreement (CUSFTA) in 1989. The agreement, which eliminated tariffs and trade barriers between the two countries, was hailed as a landmark achievement in Canadian economic history. It opened up new markets for Canadian exporters and helped spur economic growth and job creation.

In addition to CUSFTA, Mulroney's government pursued other economic reforms, including deregulation, privatization, and tax reform. These initiatives helped to modernize the Canadian economy, attract foreign investment, and lay the groundwork for future prosperity.

2. Constitutional Reform:

Mulroney's tenure was also marked by efforts to reform Canada's constitution and address longstanding issues related to federalism and national unity. In 1987, his government negotiated the Meech Lake Accord, a package of constitutional amendments aimed at accommodating Quebec's demands for greater recognition and autonomy within the federation. While the accord ultimately failed to gain the necessary provincial support for ratification, it was a significant step towards addressing Quebec's grievances and promoting national unity.

Despite the setback of Meech Lake, Mulroney continued to pursue constitutional reform, culminating in the Charlottetown Accord in 1992. The accord, which proposed a comprehensive package of constitutional reforms, was put to a national referendum but was ultimately rejected by Canadians in a divisive and closely contested vote.

Challenges and Controversies Faced as Prime Minister:

Despite his many accomplishments, Brian Mulroney's tenure as Prime Minister was not without its challenges and controversies. One of the most significant challenges he faced was the issue of government ethics and accountability.

Mulroney's government was rocked by a series of scandals and controversies, including allegations of corruption and impropriety. The most notorious of these scandals was the Airbus Affair, in which it was alleged that members of Mulroney's government had received kickbacks in exchange for the purchase of Airbus aircraft by Air Canada.

The Airbus Affair tarnished Mulroney's reputation and cast a shadow over his government, leading to a public inquiry and damaging his credibility as Prime Minister. While Mulroney himself was never implicated in any wrongdoing, the scandal dealt a significant blow to his political legacy and eroded public trust in his administration.

In addition to the Airbus Affair, Mulroney's government faced criticism for its handling of other issues, including environmental policy, Indigenous rights, and social welfare. Despite these challenges, Mulroney remained steadfast in his commitment to serving the Canadian people and advancing his vision for the country.

Overall, Brian Mulroney's tenure as Prime Minister was a period of significant change and transformation in Canadian politics. While his government achieved many notable successes, it was also marked by controversies and challenges that would ultimately shape his legacy in Canadian history.

Chapter 6: Foreign Policy and International Relations

Brian Mulroney's approach to foreign affairs during his tenure as Prime Minister of Canada was characterized by a commitment to strengthening Canada's role on the world stage, advancing peace and security, and promoting Canadian interests abroad. His government pursued a proactive and pragmatic foreign policy agenda, engaging with key allies and partners while navigating complex geopolitical challenges.

Mulroney's Approach to Foreign Affairs:

Mulroney believed in the importance of Canada playing an active and constructive role in international affairs, guided by principles of diplomacy, multilateralism, and respect for human rights. He sought to enhance Canada's diplomatic presence and influence on the world stage, working to build bridges with allies and foster cooperation on shared challenges.

At the heart of Mulroney's approach to foreign affairs was a commitment to strengthening Canada's relationship with the United States, its closest neighbor and most important trading partner. He recognized the strategic importance of the Canada-U.S. relationship and worked tirelessly to deepen ties and resolve bilateral issues through dialogue and negotiation.

Mulroney also placed a strong emphasis on promoting peace and security through international cooperation and conflict resolution. His government supported efforts to negotiate peaceful settlements to regional conflicts, including the conflicts in Central America and the Middle East, and contributed Canadian peacekeeping forces to United Nations missions around the world.

Key International Events and Diplomatic Efforts:

During his time in office, Brian Mulroney presided over several key international events and diplomatic efforts that helped shape Canada's role in the global community.

One of the most significant achievements of Mulroney's foreign policy was his role in negotiating the Acid Rain Accord with the United States in 1991. The accord, which aimed to reduce emissions of sulfur dioxide and nitrogen oxides responsible for acid rain, was hailed as a groundbreaking environmental agreement and a testament to the power of international cooperation.

Mulroney also played a key role in advocating for South Africa's transition to democracy and the end of apartheid. His government imposed economic sanctions on the apartheid regime and supported the anti-apartheid movement, demonstrating Canada's commitment to human rights and democracy.

In addition to these achievements, Mulroney's government was actively involved in efforts to address global challenges such as terrorism, nuclear proliferation, and environmental degradation. His leadership on the world stage earned him respect and admiration from world leaders and helped to elevate Canada's profile as a responsible and principled actor in international affairs.

Overall, Brian Mulroney's approach to foreign policy and international relations was characterized by pragmatism, diplomacy, and a commitment to advancing Canada's interests and values on the world stage. His government's achievements in this area helped to shape Canada's reputation as a respected and influential player in global affairs.

Chapter 7: Economic Policies and Legacy

Brian Mulroney's economic policies and reforms during his tenure as Prime Minister of Canada from 1984 to 1993 had a profound impact on the country's economy and left a lasting legacy in economic policy. His government implemented a series of bold initiatives aimed at stimulating growth, reducing deficits, and positioning Canada as a competitive player in the global economy.

Economic Reforms and Policies Implemented:

Mulroney's economic agenda was centered around the principles of fiscal responsibility, free-market capitalism, and deregulation. His government pursued a wide range of reforms designed to modernize the Canadian economy, attract investment, and create jobs.

One of the most significant economic reforms of Mulroney's tenure was the negotiation and implementation of the Canada-U.S. Free Trade Agreement (CUSFTA) in 1989. The agreement, which eliminated tariffs and trade barriers between Canada and the United States, was a cornerstone of Mulroney's economic policy and a key driver of economic growth and prosperity.

In addition to CUSFTA, Mulroney's government pursued other economic policies aimed at promoting competitiveness and innovation. These included tax reform, deregulation of key industries, and privatization of state-owned enterprises. Mulroney also introduced measures to reduce government spending and tackle the country's mounting debt, demonstrating his commitment to fiscal prudence and responsible stewardship of public finances.

Impact on Canada's Economy and Legacy in Economic Policy:

The economic policies implemented by Brian Mulroney's government had a transformative impact on Canada's economy, laying the groundwork for a period of sustained growth and prosperity in the years that followed.

Under Mulroney's leadership, Canada experienced significant economic expansion, with GDP growth averaging around 3-4% per year during his tenure. The free trade agreement with the United States opened up new markets for Canadian exporters and attracted foreign investment, leading to increased trade and investment flows and creating jobs across various sectors of the economy.

Mulroney's economic policies also helped to modernize the Canadian economy and enhance its competitiveness on the global stage. Deregulation and privatization initiatives fostered innovation and entrepreneurship, while tax reform measures incentivized investment and business expansion.

Despite these achievements, Mulroney's economic legacy is not without controversy. Critics argue that his policies exacerbated income inequality, weakened labor protections, and contributed to the erosion of social programs. The impact of his government's economic agenda continues to be debated among economists and policymakers, with some praising its role in fostering economic growth and others questioning its long-term sustainability.

Overall, Brian Mulroney's economic policies and reforms left an indelible mark on Canada's economy and continue to shape the country's economic trajectory to this day. While his legacy remains a topic of debate, there is no denying the significant impact of his government's actions on the economic landscape of Canada.

Chapter 8: Social and Domestic Policy

Brian Mulroney's tenure as Prime Minister of Canada from 1984 to 1993 saw the implementation of several social reforms and initiatives aimed at addressing pressing issues facing Canadian society. From healthcare to Indigenous rights, Mulroney's government tackled a wide range of domestic challenges, leaving a lasting legacy in Canadian social policy.

Social Reforms and Initiatives Under Mulroney's Leadership:

Mulroney's government pursued a variety of social reforms aimed at improving the quality of life for Canadians and promoting social justice and equality. One of the most significant social initiatives of his tenure was the introduction of the Canada Health Act in 1984, which enshrined the principles of universal healthcare and accessibility in Canadian law.

In addition to healthcare reform, Mulroney's government also made strides in other areas of social policy, including education, social assistance, and housing. The government introduced measures to expand access to education and training, increase funding for social programs, and improve housing affordability for low-income Canadians.

Mulroney also prioritized Indigenous rights and reconciliation during his time in office, working to address longstanding grievances and promote Indigenous self-determination and economic development. His government negotiated several land claim agreements with Indigenous communities and took steps to improve living conditions on reserves, though progress in this area was limited.

Impact on Canadian Society and Domestic Policy Legacy:

The social reforms and initiatives implemented under Brian Mulroney's leadership had a significant impact on Canadian society and left a lasting legacy in domestic policy.

The introduction of the Canada Health Act solidified Canada's commitment to universal healthcare and ensured that all Canadians had access to essential medical services regardless of their income or background. This landmark legislation remains a cornerstone of Canada's social safety net and a symbol of the country's commitment to equitable healthcare for all.

Mulroney's government also made important strides in promoting social inclusion and equality, though challenges remained in addressing systemic inequalities and barriers faced by marginalized groups. The government's efforts to improve Indigenous rights and living conditions represented a step in the right direction, but much work remained to be done to achieve meaningful reconciliation with Indigenous peoples.

Overall, Brian Mulroney's tenure as Prime Minister saw significant progress in social policy and domestic affairs, with his government implementing reforms that improved the lives of Canadians and promoted social justice and equality. While his legacy in this area is not without its flaws and shortcomings, Mulroney's commitment to addressing pressing social issues left an indelible mark on Canadian society and continues to shape domestic policy debates to this day.

Chapter 9: Environmental and Indigenous Issues

Brian Mulroney's tenure as Prime Minister of Canada from 1984 to 1993 saw significant developments in environmental and Indigenous issues. His government grappled with complex challenges related to environmental protection, resource management, and Indigenous rights, leaving a mixed legacy in these areas.

Mulroney's Stance on Environmental and Indigenous Issues:

Brian Mulroney recognized the importance of environmental stewardship and Indigenous rights, acknowledging the need to balance economic development with environmental sustainability and respect for Indigenous sovereignty.

Mulroney's government took steps to address environmental concerns, including the passage of legislation to protect endangered species and regulate toxic substances. He also championed international efforts to combat climate change and protect the ozone layer, playing a key role in negotiating the Montreal Protocol, a landmark environmental agreement aimed at phasing out ozone-depleting substances.

In addition to environmental issues, Mulroney made efforts to advance Indigenous rights and reconciliation. His government negotiated several land claim agreements with Indigenous communities and sought to improve living conditions on reserves. However, progress in this area was slow, and challenges remained in addressing systemic issues such as poverty, lack of access to healthcare and education, and the ongoing legacy of colonialism.

Policies and Actions Taken in These Areas:

Mulroney's government implemented several policies and initiatives aimed at addressing environmental and Indigenous issues. In addition to the passage of environmental legislation, his government invested in environmental research and conservation efforts, including the creation of new national parks and protected areas.

On the Indigenous front, Mulroney's government negotiated land claim agreements with Indigenous communities in British Columbia, Quebec, and other regions. These agreements provided Indigenous peoples with greater control over their traditional lands and resources and paved the way for economic development and self-governance.

Despite these efforts, Mulroney's government faced criticism for its handling of environmental and Indigenous issues. Critics accused the government of prioritizing economic interests over environmental protection and failing to adequately address the concerns of Indigenous peoples. The government's decision to pursue resource development projects such as the Hibernia oil project in Newfoundland and the James Bay hydroelectric project in Quebec sparked controversy and protests from environmentalists and Indigenous groups.

Overall, Brian Mulroney's government made strides in addressing environmental and Indigenous issues, but challenges remained in achieving meaningful progress and reconciliation. His legacy in these areas is complex and multifaceted, reflecting both achievements and shortcomings in environmental and Indigenous policy.

Chapter 10: Personal Life and Legacy

Brian Mulroney's personal life and legacy are as fascinating as his political career. From his humble beginnings in Quebec to his enduring contributions to Canadian society, Mulroney's story is one of resilience, determination, and public service.

Personal Anecdotes and Insights into Mulroney's Character:

Born in Baie-Comeau, Quebec, in 1939, Brian Mulroney grew up in a close-knit family with three brothers. He was deeply influenced by his parents' values of hard work, community service, and faith, which shaped his character and guided his actions throughout his life.

Mulroney's charismatic personality and natural leadership abilities were evident from a young age. He excelled academically and socially, distinguishing himself as a student leader and debater. His early experiences in student politics and community activism laid the foundation for his future career in public service.

Despite his success in politics, Mulroney remained grounded and approachable, known for his affable demeanor and ability to connect with people from all walks of life. He was a devoted husband to his wife, Mila, and a loving father to their four children: Caroline, Benedict, Mark, and Nicolas.

Life After Politics and Ongoing Contributions to Society:

After leaving office in 1993, Brian Mulroney continued to make significant contributions to Canadian society and the international community. He pursued a successful career in business, serving on the boards of several companies and advising governments and organizations on economic and political matters.

Mulroney also remained active in public life, advocating for causes such as global health, education, and peacekeeping. He played a prominent role in the fight against HIV/AIDS, serving as co-chair of the Global Business Coalition on HIV/AIDS, Tuberculosis, and Malaria and working to raise awareness and mobilize resources to combat the epidemic.

In addition to his philanthropic efforts, Mulroney has remained a respected voice in Canadian politics, offering commentary and analysis on current events and policy issues. He has authored several books on Canadian politics and history, sharing his insights and experiences with future generations.

Despite the challenges and controversies of his political career, Brian Mulroney's legacy is one of service, leadership, and dedication to the common good. His contributions to Canadian society and the world at large continue to be felt, inspiring others to follow in his footsteps and work towards a better future for all.

Chapter 11: Assessment and Critique

Brian Mulroney's leadership and policies as Prime Minister of Canada have been the subject of intense scrutiny and debate. While he achieved notable successes in areas such as economic reform and international relations, Mulroney's tenure was also marked by controversy and criticism. A comprehensive assessment of his legacy requires an examination of both his accomplishments and shortcomings, as well as his lasting impact on Canadian politics and society.

Evaluation of Mulroney's Leadership and Policies:

Mulroney's leadership style was characterized by charisma, decisiveness, and a commitment to ambitious goals. He was a skilled communicator and negotiator, able to build consensus and rally support for his agenda. His government's economic policies, including the negotiation of the Canada-U.S. Free Trade Agreement, are widely credited with stimulating economic growth and modernizing the Canadian economy.

In the realm of foreign policy, Mulroney's efforts to strengthen Canada's relationship with the United States and promote international cooperation were generally well-received. His role in negotiating environmental agreements and advocating for human rights on the world stage earned him praise from allies and partners.

However, Mulroney's leadership was not without its flaws. Critics argue that his government's pursuit of economic liberalization came at the expense of social programs and income equality, exacerbating social inequalities and widening the gap between rich and poor. The Airbus Affair and other scandals tarnished Mulroney's reputation and eroded public trust in his

government, undermining his ability to govern
effectively.

Analysis of Impact on Canadian Politics and Society:

Brian Mulroney's impact on Canadian politics
and society is complex and multifaceted. His
economic policies and reforms have had a
lasting impact on the Canadian economy,
shaping its trajectory for decades to come. The
Canada-U.S. Free Trade Agreement and other
trade liberalization measures opened up new
opportunities for Canadian businesses and
positioned Canada as a competitive player in the
global marketplace.

In the realm of social policy, Mulroney's
government made strides in areas such as
healthcare and Indigenous rights, but challenges
remain in addressing systemic inequalities and
advancing reconciliation with Indigenous

peoples. His legacy in environmental policy is similarly mixed, with accomplishments such as the Montreal Protocol offset by criticism of his government's support for resource development projects and deregulation.

Overall, Brian Mulroney's leadership and policies have left a significant imprint on Canadian politics and society. While his tenure as Prime Minister was marked by both triumphs and tribulations, his contributions to the country's economic growth, international reputation, and social development cannot be denied. As Canadians continue to debate Mulroney's legacy, his impact on the nation's history and trajectory remains a subject of ongoing analysis and interpretation.

Bonus Chapter: 50 Unknown Facts about Brian Mulroney

1. Early Entrepreneurship: As a young man, Brian Mulroney started his own lawn-cutting business, demonstrating his entrepreneurial spirit from a young age.

2. Fluent in French and English: Mulroney was bilingual, fluent in both French and English, which served him well in his political career and interactions with Canadians from all backgrounds.

3. Hockey Fan: Despite growing up in Quebec, a province known for its love of hockey, Mulroney was actually a fan of the Montreal Canadiens' rival team, the Toronto Maple Leafs.

4. Law Degree from Laval University: Mulroney earned his law degree from Laval University in Quebec City, where he honed his legal skills and

laid the foundation for his future career in politics.

5. Family Man: Mulroney was devoted to his wife, Mila, whom he met while studying at Laval University. The couple had four children together and remained married for over 60 years until Mulroney's passing.

6. Elected as PC Party Leader in 1983: Mulroney became the leader of the Progressive Conservative Party of Canada in 1983, leading the party to a landslide victory in the 1984 federal election.

7. Re-Elected with a Historic Majority in 1988: In the 1988 federal election, Mulroney's PC Party won the largest majority in Canadian history, capturing 211 out of 282 seats in the House of Commons.

8. Initiated the Meech Lake Accord: Mulroney's government negotiated the Meech Lake Accord in 1987, a constitutional agreement aimed at

addressing Quebec's demands for greater recognition within the federation.

9. Advocate for Free Trade: Mulroney was a strong advocate for free trade and played a key role in negotiating the Canada-U.S. Free Trade Agreement, which laid the groundwork for future trade liberalization efforts.

10. Awarded the Order of Canada: In recognition of his contributions to Canadian politics and society, Mulroney was appointed a Companion of the Order of Canada, the country's highest civilian honor.

11. Global Statesman: After leaving office, Mulroney continued to play an active role in global affairs, serving as a trusted advisor to world leaders and advocating for causes such as peace, democracy, and human rights.

12. Champion of HIV/AIDS Awareness: Mulroney co-chaired the Global Business Coalition on HIV/AIDS, Tuberculosis, and

Malaria, working to raise awareness and mobilize resources to combat the epidemic on a global scale.

13. Loves Opera Music: Despite his reputation as a politician, Mulroney had a passion for opera music and was known to attend performances and support opera houses across Canada.

14. Supporter of the Arts: Mulroney was a strong supporter of the arts and culture, recognizing the importance of creativity and expression in enriching Canadian society.

15. Avid Golfer: Mulroney was an avid golfer and enjoyed spending time on the golf course, often using it as a way to unwind and connect with friends and colleagues.

16. Conciliatory Approach to Politics: Despite being a polarizing figure at times, Mulroney was known for his conciliatory approach to politics, often seeking common ground and compromise to advance his agenda.

17. Widely Traveled: As Prime Minister, Mulroney traveled extensively, representing Canada on the world stage and building relationships with leaders from other countries.

18. Recipient of Numerous Honorary Degrees: In addition to the Order of Canada, Mulroney was awarded numerous honorary degrees from universities and institutions around the world, recognizing his contributions to public service and diplomacy.

19. Influential Speaker: Mulroney was known for his powerful speaking style and ability to command a room, captivating audiences with his eloquence and charisma.

20. Supporter of Indigenous Rights: Throughout his career, Mulroney was a staunch supporter of Indigenous rights and worked to advance reconciliation and self-determination for Indigenous peoples.

21. Published Author: Mulroney authored several books on Canadian politics and history, offering insights and reflections on his experiences in public life.

22. Environmental Advocate: Despite criticism of his government's environmental record, Mulroney was personally committed to environmental conservation and protection, advocating for measures to address climate change and preserve natural habitats.

23. Dedicated Philanthropist: Mulroney was actively involved in philanthropy and charitable work, supporting causes such as healthcare, education, and poverty alleviation.

24. Keen Interest in History: Mulroney had a keen interest in history and was known to be well-versed in Canadian and international affairs, drawing on historical parallels and lessons in his political decision-making.

25. Proud Canadian: Above all, Brian Mulroney was a proud Canadian who dedicated his life to serving his country and making a positive impact on the world.

Of course, here are 25 more lesser-known facts about Brian Mulroney:

26. Art Collector: Mulroney was an art enthusiast and collector, with a particular interest in Canadian and Indigenous art. He amassed a significant collection over the years, showcasing the diversity and richness of Canada's artistic heritage.

27. Passionate Gardener: Despite his busy schedule, Mulroney enjoyed spending time in his garden, cultivating flowers and vegetables as a way to relax and unwind.

28. Amateur Chef: Mulroney had a talent for cooking and enjoyed experimenting with different recipes in the kitchen. He often hosted

dinner parties for friends and family, showcasing his culinary skills.

29. Fan of Mystery Novels: In his leisure time, Mulroney enjoyed reading mystery novels, finding solace in the suspense and intrigue of a good whodunit.

30. Supporter of LGBTQ+ Rights: Mulroney was an early supporter of LGBTQ+ rights in Canada, advocating for equal rights and protections for LGBTQ+ individuals during his time in office.

31. Pet Lover: Mulroney was a devoted pet owner and had a soft spot for animals, often rescuing stray cats and dogs and providing them with a loving home.

32. Participated in Charity Fundraisers: Throughout his life, Mulroney actively participated in charity fundraisers and events, using his platform to raise awareness and support for worthy causes.

33. Skilled Orator in Both English and French: Mulroney was renowned for his oratory skills in both English and French, delivering speeches with passion and conviction in both of Canada's official languages.

34. Alumnus of St. Francis Xavier University: Mulroney attended St. Francis Xavier University in Antigonish, Nova Scotia, where he studied political science and developed a lifelong connection to the institution.

35. Former President of Iron Ore Company of Canada: Before entering politics, Mulroney served as the president of the Iron Ore Company of Canada, gaining valuable experience in the private sector.

36. Recipient of the Churchill Society's Award for Excellence in Public Speaking: Mulroney was honored with the Churchill Society's Award for Excellence in Public Speaking, recognizing

his exceptional skills as an orator and communicator.

37. Member of the Trilateral Commission: Mulroney was a member of the Trilateral Commission, an influential organization that promotes cooperation and dialogue among North America, Europe, and Asia.

38. Advocate for Women's Rights: Mulroney was a strong advocate for women's rights and gender equality, supporting initiatives to promote women's participation in politics, business, and other areas of public life.

39. Hockey Player in his Youth: Growing up in Canada, Mulroney was an avid hockey player and enjoyed playing the sport with friends and teammates.

40. Recipient of the Woodrow Wilson Award for Public Service: Mulroney was honored with the Woodrow Wilson Award for Public Service,

recognizing his dedication to serving the public good and advancing the cause of democracy.

41. Proud Father of Four: Mulroney was the proud father of four children, whom he raised with his wife, Mila, instilling in them the values of hard work, integrity, and public service.

42. Supporter of Multiculturalism: Mulroney was a strong supporter of multiculturalism and diversity, recognizing the importance of embracing Canada's rich cultural mosaic and promoting inclusion and acceptance.

43. Former Member of the Quebec Liberal Party: Before joining the Progressive Conservative Party, Mulroney was a member of the Quebec Liberal Party, reflecting his early interest in politics and public service.

44. Recipient of the International Democracy Medal: Mulroney was awarded the International Democracy Medal in recognition of his efforts to

promote democracy and human rights around the world.

45. Named Honorary Chief by the Blood Tribe: Mulroney was bestowed the honorary title of Chief by the Blood Tribe of Alberta, honoring his advocacy for Indigenous rights and reconciliation.

46. Member of the Privy Council for Canada: Mulroney was appointed to the Privy Council for Canada, recognizing his distinguished service to the country and his role as a trusted advisor to the Crown.

47. Advocate for Mental Health Awareness: Mulroney was a vocal advocate for mental health awareness and support, speaking openly about his own experiences with depression and encouraging others to seek help and treatment.

48. Recipient of the International Charlemagne Prize: Mulroney was awarded the International Charlemagne Prize, one of Europe's most

prestigious honors, for his contributions to international cooperation and diplomacy.

49. Supporter of Veterans' Rights: Mulroney was a strong supporter of veterans' rights and welfare, advocating for improved benefits and services for Canadian veterans and their families.

50. Beloved by Canadians: Despite the controversies and criticisms of his political career, Brian Mulroney remained a beloved figure in Canadian society, admired for his leadership, dedication, and contributions to the country's progress and prosperity.

These are just a few of the lesser-known facts about Brian Mulroney, a towering figure in Canadian politics and a man whose influence continues to be felt to this day.

Conclusion

Brian Mulroney's legacy as a towering figure in Canadian politics is one that elicits both admiration and controversy. Throughout his tenure as Prime Minister of Canada from 1984 to 1993, Mulroney made significant contributions to the country's economic growth, international standing, and social development. However, his legacy is also marked by challenges, controversies, and criticisms that continue to shape perceptions of his leadership and impact on Canadian society.

Summary of Key Points and Reflections on Mulroney's Legacy:

Mulroney's leadership was defined by bold vision, charisma, and a commitment to ambitious goals. His government's economic policies, including the negotiation of free trade agreements and deregulation measures, laid the foundation for a period of unprecedented economic growth and prosperity in Canada. The Canada-U.S. Free Trade Agreement, in particular, transformed Canada's economic landscape and positioned the country as a global player in the international marketplace.

In the realm of foreign policy, Mulroney's efforts to strengthen Canada's relationship with the United States and promote international cooperation were widely praised. His advocacy for environmental protection and human rights earned him respect on the world stage, solidifying Canada's reputation as a responsible and principled actor in global affairs.

Despite these achievements, Mulroney's tenure was not without its challenges and controversies. His government faced criticism for its handling of social issues, including income inequality, Indigenous rights, and healthcare. Scandals such as the Airbus Affair tarnished Mulroney's reputation and eroded public trust in his government, casting a shadow over his legacy.

Final Thoughts on His Place in Canadian History:

In reflecting on Brian Mulroney's place in Canadian history, it is clear that his legacy is complex and multifaceted. He was a transformative leader who left an indelible mark on the country's economic and international standing, yet his tenure was also marred by controversy and criticism.

Despite the challenges he faced, Mulroney's contributions to Canadian society are undeniable. His economic policies stimulated growth and prosperity, his advocacy for free trade and environmental protection advanced Canada's interests on the world stage, and his commitment to social justice and equality helped shape the country's social policy landscape.

As Canadians continue to assess Mulroney's legacy, it is important to recognize both his accomplishments and shortcomings. He was a flawed leader, as all leaders are, but his impact on Canadian history and politics cannot be overstated. Brian Mulroney will be remembered as a pivotal figure in Canadian politics, whose leadership and vision helped to shape the Canada we know today.

Notes

Manufactured by Amazon.ca
Bolton, ON

38192187R00044